"I was following. But what was I following? With a frail, tilted structure in the air, I joined in the grand and noble exalting adventure of elucidating the Universe in its entirety."

Henri Michaux, from *Grasp*
translation by Richard Sieburth

DECOHERENT
DE'GNIW EHT

Elizabeth

Zuba

SplitLevel Texts

Albert

Hugh

Niels

Act One

Afternoon tea.

A drawing room.

The distant sound of a cat scratching at a larder.

Albert (jocund, greying mustache, tweed suit) and Niels (lanky, hair combed flat, more pensive) are deep in conversation.

Hugh (feathered) peers in through a window.

Albert: ... Really! Absolute heaps of fleecy honeysuckles, and we made
no attempt to shear them. Wolfgang said it must have been the
way the honeysuckles cried for Truth to come save them, deposit
them in the amplest nook it might find and then hop o'er the near
stream in search of the young forester and his lover deeper in
the woods, talking plaintively in low voices under the nestled fowl
family perched —

Niels: Fowl family?

Albert: Chickens, yes, perched in the nearby spruce tree — But come
come, don't look so worried, Niels! Truth did find them in the
end, the forester and his lover I mean ... though not, it should be
said, before overhearing first a bit of their conversation ... Oh what
was it again, something about a feather ... or a hand —

Niels: They could have put a wing in the chasm's side, but no, it was my
lung.

Niels?

(That's Hugh, far right, outside the window)

A wing?

Who can say, mein freund.

And the lung?

Damn if I know, all these branching passages, breath and eyebright —

Like the light behind the surprise of every morning milk-yellow somewhere
pasturing clans in the fold. All of a sudden (even for themselves) pasturing
in the fold.

... Where, even now, one might nicker and nuzzle his mouth into the grass,
stir bird-heft out from his nostrils into the morning fog, and then
lift his head and twitch his ears at a sound plucked from a hill beyond,
where, over that hill, down the river, behind the fast-holding bank vegetation,
shrubs and foxtail and such, a boy rises from the bank, stands quietly
for a time, then lifts his arm, his hand, and waves the river down.

yes

(Hugh mouths at the window)
yes

you had tucked
your fingers into your sash
by then,
waiting by the coppices
to be followed by much less,
we thumped the ground
for its milky dew

remember?

(and mimes a thumping motion)

A feather in the river swift along the river, no depths in its voyage but for the trace of a touching. Befindlichkeit, brother, and sweetly.

You mean other wing mechanics?

Or otherwhere vectors where we watch our yellow toes point as they near ground ...

So about that fowl family —

Against the mathematical gulch, the covenants. The child. The 5000 years. The child AGAIN.

If the sun has ever wondered why chickens seldom lay their heads on porches for shelter, I present my lily back. In the distance, a shimmering silhouette descends the far hills. Hard to say if it is one man or two from here, but descend it does. Quick now, prepare the hearth, the tea ... My God, Albert. I fear the chickens have heard me. Look how they line up in pairs and thrust out far their necks.

And say of their kin,

between the hand and the wing, the feather may sleep,

The hand and the wing being sleep of another.

The clods of earth in the distance, the dense flocks passing.

And yet ... miniaturizing the larger birds did as little for the landscape

as the superposition of a single piece of coffee

(is not splendor) or the migrating oxen

laid heavy at last on their Northern haunches, taking the cud softly

into the corners of their mouths, their mouths charmingly twisted

as if to say — And did we run away?

No, no we did not.

As if to say, you are a roving eye of expanding feathered density,
sometimes full with, sometimes empty of matter ...

Yes, but which among me am I?

...

And if it isn't *am* to leave thee thus?

(Hugh stretches long his neck
and lays his cheek against the window)

But really, I must <u>know</u>, somehow <u>know,</u> which among me plays an
accordion number under a trestle bridge somewhere, folding jubilantly in
the whitewashed flocks, whooping in and out, sleepwalking lest I appear
so tremblingly natural, presenting the bridge folk with the town scepter
I'd run down from the hills, passing the rains, the fig tree, the oriole
hungry at its base, what was permitted and plotted for the oriole, might the
accordions have veiled less their hands in my own.

...where the fluctuate
dleif eht ssorca sparw
and time emerges
wolp a
a plow

$\delta_x \delta_p \geq \frac{\hbar}{2}$ The sleepy bear in his elephant cave (the sag and buckle, the grasses shoving in and out both ends) and the crushed grasses in his paws held out to show the crushed grasses. $\delta_x \delta_p \geq \frac{\hbar}{2}$

OK, just for argument's sake, let's say this "muscatel" who is also
one of the big bazoomers (nothing ever being all that other after all)
went for a stroll through a daisy patch, a dandelion field,
a second daisy patch, another dandelion field and laid down
on the banks of the Green Gates believing he had at long last
found his best gesture of immortality.
Yes, the bazoomers will say,
the more invisible the better.
All of us.
O you bearers of bearing, O you makers of the earth,
my bed of moss is a work of remembering.

So it is, we agree, and take watch upon the clover.

The way a sparrow wintering in a tree will roll a little toward the fog when it comes in and then roll back and a little away.

... But if by observer we meant something more complex and automatic?

And listen where no score
worth a hill of beans sounds
less than its angels. I keep a copy here
in my breast pocket, said the boy
on the field begging room on the field
for a slender boy like me. The time is nigh, men.
The rams batter at the city gates.
The breastplates and the blossoming fruit trees.
The standards and the oiled horns.
The thoughtful ambulatory verse-making drifting up
and then down over the hill, first legless,
then middleless, then their tribe of heads floating out.
Travel'd thro this winged effigy of our breed at their shields.

(and mimes the thumping a little again)

All intentions by one reason, who could ever comfort
so solitary a solitary bleat behind a barn wall despite
the recent light showers, as dry as ever? Altogether, Albert, bleating
feels almost always like it's keeping you in one place, across the lea.
I must write to Werner and tell him about passion and its edging
along the chaotic, today I saw a stone wall stuck to hollyhocks
stuck to an apricot tree stuck to a darling cat stuck to peat moss
stuck to an arbor of privet stuck to a little blue courtyard
stuck to a mouth that has no eyes to follow
its wounds like the petticoat, the satchel, the mask,
for the whole reason a wall like that begins in the first place.

You know, the paths really do feel as familiar as one's. The paths really do feel as familiar as one's own cavity humming lightly on one's own. own cavity humming. own knees. The paths really do feel as familiar as one's own cavity humming lightly on one's own knees. The paths really do feel as familiar as one's own cavity humming lightly on one's own knees. knees. lightly on one's —

Enough.

But can you hear in the shaft?

The fluctuate shaft?

The bleating keeping you in one place,

the blinking date palms, the solitary squawk,

the great sky whinny, the doubling tail-angels.

Or not sounds, per se, but the waving.

The fleet of fishing boat lanterns across a sphere

that must be made once the mold is removed,

barely dry enough to hold its shape.

A bat drops down and presses lightly its bat print. Firmer now. Quieter.

Traveled thro this wing'ed effigy

And let us not forget that on the day of precautionary measures,
the children go out from their houses by the four winds,
measuring a distance of thirty paces and gathering the grasses, earth,
gravel they find there. With these, the bounty of the thirty paces,
they return along the same paths and feed them to the elders,
later launching them off as human canoes into
the great aqueducts that circle the city by a shifting gradation
that permits their continuous current, volleying us
on to where we wave ourselves home.
…Voilà! The surface of interior!

Where no other light will do.

(Hugh scratches out a little bunker,
sits back and lights a cigarette)

And yet, having conceded all haptic counsel ...
extant and haptic counsel ... how little remains for the coming atom.
I took watch and waited for time to show
me something I could not have expected.
Do you remember it?
The gentle sway, the tender nothing, the nunc stans?

Barely.

Yes. Me too ...

Come, Niels, there are purple snails to boil for the kings' robes and cedar logs to cast adrift (arms tight around them, seaweed throbbing at our sides) the very logs we'll use for the gates of the city when we at last arrive. We'll erect two posts and hollow a length-wise hole into one side of each door and in this way fashion the gates to open inward and outward toward the swelling throngs. You're probably right about letting them pour in and out that way, and how lost we'd be without the great cedar forests.

Take instead the field that look, Hurrah, does yet wave its tired field hands.
Take instead the silhouetteless sky stroking its many parts their endless
undergrowths.

Undergrowths like nothing I can imagine my hands.

Like the last little sheep that was really a father bleating everything,
meaning the ground of the brain,
out over the meadow, along the barn walls, into the silo,
where at last a single ant, if not more, pauses to accept it,
for if an ant hopes for anything it is a circular room
with endless aisles, a soft bosom, a morsel or two.

                                                              Ay.
                                                              Ay.

                                        (looking out at the annular walls,
                                        Hugh lays his crown on the pyre
                                        and lets fall his body upon it)

                                                    Each sound
                                        from the sheep's throat
                                        carries on this way.

Carry on. Wait —

Carry on.

The way a lob of a wriggling bird on the fire hails the harvest. You angle
your head through the crowd and bid it a farewell of sorts — Bird, I bear
you neither mausoleum, the cracks and crumble that would later overtake
it, nor passage by Charon. Blessed are those winging heavenbound of
bulging nares and crying "Perfect Hogwash, Ye Mortals!", circling the
circle that drops its wet jaw and groans, beak pressed against the circle
window, bound to its matter as much as the matter by which it moves. And
the weather today as calm, mild, as early April.

Craggy heights and slender seeds our chests

in the great sky-jaw heave like stars be they suns,

not yet gone dark, not yet, not completely.

Stopping by to remind the crickets of the cricket we left

as ballast against our unease, shaking at its shaking

at trying to point anywhere.

It troubles me, Albert.

The bounty upon their backs troubles me.

The angels on their lower legs like that, the air they hang from,

the so few to witness hangings generally.

Brambling and buckeye —

Hard to say which part of the bird is the tree and which part are the feathers in your eye from here ... Or, rather, not the history in the bird, but all the people.

And if the people of the blur are not the blur?

But what we wave.
See your faces?

To make an enamel of hyacinth

A slippery outblooming enamel.

Did I tell you that young fellow Hugh sent a postcard, bunker steps and saskatoon pie? Thought his parcel might be emotionally unpopulated, he said, in origin, but then more populated in creation. Something about the yellow commons and birch-shaded hollows where we bent our steps toward the waterside and made our way further into the rustling light around the golden birth like lambs milkjoicing.

The wild pines shuttling the winds onward.

Yes, and the birds flattening sometimes.

Beating vigorously their wings.

Still a while.

Then beating again.

Like when I step in and look up at the branch from beneath it, it flattens and hovers, and the sky distances. Stepping back a couple paces, the sky drops down and the branch rises.

So what? Will the bramble not arrange itself according to dimension or octave? Bepetal not the undergrowth, birdsong not the confinement?

Were a hillock ever an hour or a bated cheek against the sun?

(Hugh, plucking a passing bird from the ether
and lobbing it onto the fire)

Selah.
Huang Di must have paced
countless nights in his silk robe
watching for the next deluge, ark, animals in pairs —
and all from such different lands —
parting clean the space-time, floating into port,
felling open the hatch. Boiled in the empress's tea.
Cocoons unraveled shiny and infinite,
almost invisible.

I can't see.

...Toy animals, you are welcome here.
Your nimble ankles. Your short lifted tails
making tail-angels in the living
room air space. The swathing of shapes
on restless elements. I like to think
of our shared habit of desperation
as middle earth. An arc-like shape
drifting over a parachute held by a ring
of children, an armature of feathers,
already their own arc,
that need not be transformed to give
them wing. And as the evening goes on,
the time-lapsed sound of a whipping propeller
begins to fill my mouth. Mouth
with you.

(But how DID the gentle goat picture break up into grunts and whistles and song?,
whispers Wolfgang up to Hugh)

The heavy date palms.
The clay vessel on the bank.
Nothing that the goat says.

All the nannies and kids leaning over the fence, beautiful souls, braying
at the spaniel flushed from the brush. Spaniel! Spaniel! Send forth your
golden blossoms so spirited and ungeographic!

Interfere, Wolfgang.

Swab with your bare hands

Just look at Chico there,
bending low his dog forehead
over the wings beating to ascend the first
perhaps the second tree limb, no more.
None needed.
Some say masks though they fit no face.
Anyway, he's turned the birds
some billion times round the field by now
where we wait to wait nowhere else ...
waving. volleying. face blindness.

Across the field

.elbisivid era ew

Albert, your spongy tree beckons hungry, buck-toothed mammal friends.
Adjusts perceptibly the posture of other organisms. The way of regard and
positioning, the loose tremble of a single sprig of wheat in a maiden's ear,
I nestle my head at your bulging roots, cast my cheek in their embeddable
mass — O Mammal friends. Go out. Lay your heads in the laps of men who
bend like tree limbs by little reason.

Even Pan paused on his way to the river to drink from the nymphs' raised
palms, paused and listened for the scrap scurry. "Time enough to look for
those lil' buggers later," he mutters.

Obviously Pan has never had an infestation.

A spongy infestation. Come, let us speak
of the wall behind Breton's desk, of Monet's lilies
and their like, beset by their place in history. O!
Or better still, hold hands and run like a god-lion
across the night sky. I will not say that with us, the branches
lifted briefly from their shoulders but inasmuch I am keeping
something from you. A rounded sleep under stuttering branch light.
A shifting grassy route under a wide grassy plain.
Once again a reminder that a mulberry tree is rarely the place
of mulberry tree histories. And once again
a reminder of how slow I was to see it.

Painting a bull's-eye on the beach
got quite a game of egg-toss going.

Sometimes my right wing still flutters
mid-air
in expectation.

Then mops my brow.

Hummm.

(now humming a little hummy tune)

I've been meaning to ask if you see my hands in my hands?

Yes.

Fitly breached from any human pair descending a mountain?

For what has the eye of Imagination been bestowed upon man if not for the ungainly, chicken?

Where a fetid dust floats out over
Accelerator Island, high above the buried
chipmunk nests, the wasps, the moles,
the singers that serenade us while we bathe
and anoint ourselves with matter beyond us,
taking close these pastimes, winking along
with the young sailor's sextant and the dust up
ahead assuming its rich golden hue, led and not led
to water, glistens, returns all light,
sends knots out like its long lost mane,
sends knots out like men who measure time and space
by knots, sends crowns for the dancers dancing.

No rising sea can stay my small falling wings.

Proportions but fail the reverent, Albert. I slip back into my cave,
its cave mouth window slung over my face like bestial haunches come the
flood of rippling light, the very one for whom the sea ought to be rising.

Somewhere, the tidal line carries on along the beach thinking: new lagoons.

Still, it was enough for the goldfinch
to spirit his palsied cheek, lil' bloomer,
rubbing it fast as finch be
against the tree,
no intercourse ever burdened so little
any other enormous yellow ...

.wolp a egreme yam emit

Yes, yes, like after looking at an image for some time,
how it will begin to quake, having shifted its gaze.

Hummm.

And yet, things may not be what they contain either.

Carrying father goat, he had his arms around us and we held him in a sitting position.

The circle dropped off where I lifted my scythe to the edge of the wheat and reappeared in a perfect radius on the other side.

Sitting in the enumerated heather of the moorlands,
we imagined an occasional passing red grouse
and then listened for him. Remember? Listen.
Some say the grouse would say, pay no attention and listen,
I have a gift for your ancestors, I have seen nothing
but occasion and it moves us like Chesterton the skeleton.

So, you have seen it too, one existing by the other ...

Oooo PIFFLE. Ever since Werner left and didn't open his palm to the pear tree, you've been promising lush coppices to the stars and long precipitated coppice peninsulas who would compose them even in taking note of composing them — bind-thyself-to-a-joy kind of binding ... I'm suddenly taken here with explaining the trouble with quadrilles shifting too gaily in the Holly Grove. Some reduce emptiness with fullers, friend, but others, others stay thin.

Massless   Massive

(*Uncertain, Hugh*
stoops and bares
his teeth
at the brook)

Like the child who laid his head on the refrigerator
and hummed the minuet, the part of the oboe,
the purr, the warm embrace, the dish on the floor.
Just the two of us, they said, and prepared
for the coming rift between their chamber
and their hum ...

Listen, we have two maps and yours looks like a lion. No lion has ever
led a man to a honeycomb or bit a finger for the dire gold before but true
north has given way to a fatter sun that we might call the Queen of Light's
Chariot trampling multitudes at the behest of her quadrupeds' irrational
fear of any pivot-point turns where the darker shades of the gorgeous
nothings rustle, so that if we feed my map to your lion, he could get a whole
new horizon, free.

                                              Free, chickens!

                                           Everything for
                                                  which
                                              compose
                                                   the
                                                sunset
                                                  keep

Cutting the no-man's land to the quick, the horse sent out a horse with a no-man's flag. Naturally, said the horse, without it, no-man wouldn't exist. Later, I held him close to my breast and patted firm his chin.

It's getting late ...

The time has come to take comfort in window structures at the hour of the sunset, the muted light reflected casually on our foreheads chatting here over tea. The same way we might languidly yodel inside boxes. Leydeeyodelleyhee.

Yodeling gestures sometimes startle from human-size boxes.

Funny, I once told Kirchoff no rabbit had ever followed _me_ home and as the rabbit's from the carrot-family, he could never know any better anyhow.

Whatever will we do with another carrot portraiture, rabbits?

He giveth, he taketh away. The art of nativity is of less import every day. Somewhere a native head crops up from beyond the distant hill — Look! It's Kirchoff come back.

Niels, Niels, it's all in the field. Cutting its field-trough edges up from the bank to the native houses. Across the way, a quarrelsome pair rests between worlds, quietly pleasured in their spare breathing, an almost natural view of things where the water springs up and wild geese like the verdant drapery that never crawls right up to the paths, smooth and dry and retired as they are.

My spool in the soft river where the wind stretches over.
I pluck the ripened touchreel from its precision,
it splits volume where I nick my finger.

(Hugh leans in close to his reflection
in the window and pats firm his chin)

I say we make volume an apiary. A humming humming sky.
The drones below fighting upwardly tooth and nail
a biddable lattice to be leapt from yet and leaping,
not to mention the honey and hot biscuits.
Into brittle flakes, the weighty wafer,

> Yes Yes!
> Honey and hot biscuits!
> We must prepare ourselves to be taken with us.

to betake us.

And Saint Denis, who walked six miles with his head in his terrace
hand looking out over Paris. Ithaca at last, by its slow reduction from
its own sails, breaking touched to be touched like the single occasional
note through the grass symphony overrun by a solitary delicacy. (Both
symphony and solitary delicacy. By way of neither. A reasonable dream.)
Whereof one cannot speak, one must pass over in silence, and with a
flourish of my arm, I set to running between the forest and the clearing
in my best manner of confiscation. The leaves stirred though one could
not say rustled, and other peculiarities were the theme song from The
Greatest American Hero that echoed in the canopy and the bird barracks
that defined the path.

Or the people of Mount Ouef roped to a doorframe in the middle of the field but resist this by running in fast circles around the frame, who, from a distance, because of their speed, give the familiar appearance of a solid mound.

Today, the birdsong is a low achromatic dirge but not I hope tomorrow if music changes its tonality by its surroundings.

Who wishes his song be analyzed for its sad neuroses rather than responded to like a call?

Songs where the fairywren calls wide from the throat. The feather redder in the road than at her lilted haunches.

Leading a horse to a stream, a mother gazing out at her child, a ditch in the shape of a bearskin rug where the dirt's been left piled where its head should be, like it's eaten the rest of him. A quiet taxidermy. The dust upon duration. Running fast into a jar's mouth insofar as one bows one's head.

Albert, you barely remember yourself! Wherefore gone your swinging tail and elevator lips? Your whinny? I'm wont to advise poise but what god hath eaten your portrait? Refute all portraits, friend. Refute all portraits and their people. Even in the damp night, when you lean gently over your fireside and wait naturally there — refute this.

Because human sense(s) gloss over smaller scales, my arrow fell to the
earth in Delaware ...

The grass seldom lets the wind do what it was intended to do (be followed
like tigers know better)
and knots itself into animal shapes.

Yes ... it made a whispering sound I could not hear but imagined ...

Before you go, what say we send a message out to the cloned creatures of
the world?

Quite right.

Cloned creatures, take my hand to your
snouts. Ahead the petals ruffle and fluff on
the bough. The birds' solitary squawk and
plentiful hills. The cloak over the branch
and the trembling cloak. Wherever I go,
the wavelength breaks before me.
Which means I move to keep things breaking.
Makes so much more sense.
As when lovers are reunited, God bless this meal.

The horse has no knees after all,
to spook by,
sayeth the river now gliding along
imperceptibly
on tip-toes
where attentive quadrupeds return
its every whinny,
where a mere 3.1 miles out
our every possible dream awaits.
maerD. There, on the horizon,
all beauty ever lain at our hooves,
the whole damn Critique of the Sublime.

(pressing his open mouth hard against the window)

The other day Wolfgang said one could make an argument that prayer is the most intimate poetry of all, being many places other than itself.

Amen.   Amen.

(steaming mouth-clouds on the glass)

All feathers drained from the canopy.
A shelter materializes out of a shelter
floating swift along the surface.

Beaming up steadily your sometimes retina atoms,
we wave the river down.

Your right wing, high, lyre-less, like a blind lyre-sabateour
traveled
thro

... following the natural thread
engulfing the last 3-dimensional glades,
the sum and substance behind them.
All the verdure of light where the passage
turns something extractable.
An aria one might say.
Informationettas are little wise here and inseparable
from the ballads played above their heads,
calling to each other choppy water cries
across the flat horizon, carrying shiploads of costumed singers
past the distracted farmers up along the hills,
the day-dreaming shepherds, the willowy schools of weary children
too young to know that there really is a baby-delivery stork,
that there really are storks of which we are part
and they ought not to feel so deceived.
Storks of which we are part and their heavy stork heads,
their heavy stork heads
at our shoulders.

Greening light up the fishwing buoys,

we mouth to the passing clouds.

Come.

We mouth

htrof dna kcab

back and forth a chamber over the light.

Curtain.

ACKNOWLEDGEMENTS

This book is dedicated to Quito Zuba. And fellow chickens Emmeline and Sebastian.

And to the great madcaps of quantum physics, particularly Niels Bohr, Albert Einstein (and their famed debates), Hugh Everett III, Wolfgang Pauli, Werner Heisenberg, and Gustav Kirchoff, among others, who never cease to astonish and whose vertiginous discoveries and personalities traverse these pages, however loosely.

My deep and unrepayable debt to SplitLevel Texts for believing in this book; and particularly to Karla Kelsey for her indomitable energy and unparalleled insight.

Thank you to my friends for all things life and wonder; most especially Jen Bervin, the wing'ed.

The following poems are for:

Jen Bervin, "As if to say" and "Listen, we have two maps" ("which/ compose/the/sunset/keep" is E. Dickinson, A821)

Danniel Schoonebeek, "All intention by one reason," "Did I tell you that young Hugh" and "The other day Wolfgang"

Andrew Beccone, "Or the way a lob of a wriggling bird"

Uljana Wolf, "Just look at Chico there" ("face blindness" is from Uljana's poem *Analogue on Flowers,* translated by Sophie Seita)

Catherine McCrae, "Sitting in the enumerated heather" (Chesterton lives with her)

Ray Johnson, "Oooo PIFFLE." and "Because human sense(s) gloss"

Christian Hawkey, "Like the child who laid his head" and "Let's make volume an apiary"

Marcel Broodthaers, "Or the people of Mount Ouef"

ELIZABETH ZUBA

Elizabeth Zuba is the author of *Decoherent The Wing'ed,* the chapbook *May Double as a Whistle* (Song Cave Press, 2015), and the critical work *Ray Johnson's Art World* (Feigen Gallery, 2014). She is the editor of *Not Nothing: Selected Writings by Ray Johnson 1954-1994* (Siglio Press, 2014); and translator and co-editor of *Marcel Broodthaers: My Ogre Book Shadow Theater Midnight* (Siglio Press, 2015) and *La Familia Americana,* an anthology of contemporary American poetry (Cosmopoética: Madrid, 2010). Elizabeth has co-translated (with Maria Gilissen) several of Marcel Broodthaers's books and writings, including *Pense-Bête* (Granary Book, 2016), *10,000 Francs Reward* (Printed Matter, 2016), and *En lisant la Lorelei* (for the Museum of Modern Art, 2016).

SPLITLEVEL TITLES

Laynie Browne, *PRACTICE*
Martin Corless-Smith, *This Fatal Looking Glass*
Alan Gilbert, *The Treatment of Monuments*
Carla Harryman, *W—/M—*
Lucy Ives, *The Worldkillers*
Bernadette Mayer, *The Desires of Mothers to Please Others in Letters*
Catherine Meng, *The Longest Total Solar Eclipse of the Century*
Jerome Rothenberg, *A Cruel Nirvana*
Maged Zaher, *If Reality Doesn't Work Out*
Elizabeth Zuba, *Decoherent The Wing'ed*

 SplitLevel Texts

SplitLevel Texts
Urbana, Illinois 61801
http://www.splitleveltexts.com

Copyright © 2016 Elizabeth Zuba
Printed in the United States of America
Cover design by Kevin Woodland

ISBN: 978-0-9858111-8-1

Library of Congress Control Number: 2016937691